ESCUE RIDERS

FIRE TRUCKS TO THE RESCUE!

BY FRANCES NAGLE

Gareth Stevens
PUBLISHING

Please visit our website, www.garethstevens.com. For a free color catalog of all our high-quality books, call toll free 1-800-542-2595 or fax 1-877-542-2596.

Library of Congress Cataloging-in-Publication Data
Names: Nagle, Frances, author.
Title: Fire trucks to the rescue! / Frances Nagle.
Description: New York : Gareth Stevens Publishing, [2023] | Series: Rescue riders | Includes index.
Identifiers: LCCN 2021046772 (print) | LCCN 2021046773 (ebook) | ISBN 9781538278529 (set) | ISBN 9781538278536 (library binding) | ISBN 9781538278512 (paperback) | ISBN 9781538278543 (ebook)
Subjects: LCSH: Fire engines–Juvenile literature. | Fire extinction–Juvenile literature.
Classification: LCC TH9372 .N34 2023 (print) | LCC TH9372 (ebook) | DDC 628.9/259–dc23/eng/20211115
LC record available at https://lccn.loc.gov/2021046772
LC ebook record available at https://lccn.loc.gov/2021046773

Published in 2023 by
Gareth Stevens Publishing
29 E. 21st Street
New York, NY 10010

Portions of this work were originally authored by B. J. Best and published as *Fire Trucks*. All new material this edition authored by Frances Nagle.

Designer: Leslie Taylor
Editor: Kristen Nelson

Photo credits: Cover temp-64GTX/Shutterstock.com; pp. 2-24 (background texture) Pixel Embargo/Shutterstock.com; p. 5 Terry Poche/Shutterstock.com; p. 7 (top) Wangkun Jia/Shutterstock.com; p. 7 (bottom) EQRoy/Shutterstock.com; p. 9 Tyler Olson/Shutterstock.com; p. 11 blurAZ/Shutterstock.com; p. 13 Gorodenkoff/Shutterstock.com; p. 15 (inset) New Africa/Shutterstock.com; p. 15 Christine Bird/Shutterstock.com; p. 17 Mike Brake/Shutterstock.com; p. 19 Kletr/Shutterstock.com; p. 21 Monkey Business Images/Shutterstock.com.

Printed in the United States of America

CPSIA compliance information: Batch #CSGS23: For further information contact Gareth Stevens, New York, New York at 1-800-542-2595.

CONTENTS

Boldface words appear in the glossary.

Building on Fire!

Smoke starts to pour from the windows of a building. It's a fire! It's time to call the fire department. The firefighters are trained to come fast. They drive a big truck that gets them to the fire. It's a fire truck!

Fire trucks are emergency **vehicles**. An emergency is a **dangerous** or unexpected **situation**. Fire trucks are painted bright colors. This makes them easy for people to spot. Most fire trucks are red. They can also be yellow.

CAMBRIDGE FIRE
E3
CAMBRIDGE
ENGINE 3
ENG3INE

63
CHICAGO - O'HARE
63
TOWER CO.
CHICAGO FIRE DEPT.
63

On Call

When firefighters get a call, they put on **protective** gear. It includes a helmet, or hard hat, to keep their head safe. Firefighters can get a fire truck ready and be on the road in minutes.

Fire trucks have loud sirens. They have flashing lights too. Firefighters put on the siren and lights to tell cars to get out of the way. They drive the fire truck to an emergency fast.

TRUCK

More than Fighting Fires

Fire trucks are called to all kinds of emergencies. They go to house or building fires. They are also called to car crashes. Firefighters can open crashed cars. Fire trucks often arrive when someone is very hurt or sick. Firefighters have **medical** training to help.

VP

What's in the Truck?

There are many tools on a fire truck. There are axes and ladders to use during fires. Fire trucks have **radios**. Firefighters use these to talk to one another during an emergency. They talk to other trucks nearby. Fire trucks have medical supplies too.

Fire & Rescue Service

Kinds of Truck

There are a few kinds of fire truck. A pumper has big hoses. It gets water from a **fire hydrant**. Firefighters use the hoses and water to put out the fire. Pumpers also carry water in a tank.

ENGINE

Ladder trucks have a tall ladder on top. It may be up to 100 feet (30.5 m) tall! Firefighters climb the ladder with hoses. They spray water on a fire. They use the ladder to **rescue** people.

To the Rescue!

Firefighters are community helpers with a dangerous job. They're called to emergencies to help people and save buildings. They need fast trucks to get to emergencies quickly. Fire trucks are important emergency vehicles!

MEDICAL
SERVICES

GLOSSARY

dangerous: unsafe

fire hydrant: a pipe commonly in the street that has water especially used for putting out fires

medical: having to do with care given by doctors or other healthcare workers

protective: having to do with keeping safe

radio: a device that is used to send and receive messages by radio

rescue: to free a person or thing from unsafe conditions

situation: the conditions and events happening at a certain time and place

vehicle: an object that moves people from one place to another

FOR MORE INFORMATION

BOOKS

Harris, Bizzy. *Fire Trucks*. Minneapolis, MN: Jump!, Inc., 2022.

Rossiter, Brienna. *Big Machines for Fire and Rescue*. Lake Elmo, MN: Focus Readers, 2021.

WEBSITE

What to Do in a Fire
kidshealth.org/en/kids/fire-safety.html

Be prepared for a fire using fire safety tips like these!

Publisher's note to educators and parents: Our editors have carefully reviewed these websites to ensure that they are suitable for students. Many websites change frequently, however, and we cannot guarantee that a site's future contents will continue to meet our high standards of quality and educational value. Be advised that students should be closely supervised whenever they access the internet.

INDEX